acknowledgements

Sections of this work have previously been published in the following periodicals – *The Journal*, *Pennine Platform* and *Other Poetry.*

The author would also like to thank the following, snippets from whose work form parts of the title sequence: Mikhail Ardov, Margaret Atwood, Lesley Chamberlain, Terry Eagleton and James Hamilton-Paterson. Also embedded in a number of poems are one or more shards from work by Theodor Adorno, Charles Baudelaire, Samuel Beckett, Paul Celan, Martin Heidegger, James Joyce, Robert Lowell, F.W.Nietzsche, Wallace Stevens, Alexander Trocchi and William Wordsworth.

Peninsula

Peter Loney

BeWrite Books
www.bewrite.net

Published internationally by BeWrite Books, Canada.
208 – 19897, 56th Avenue, Langley, BC, V3A 3Y1.

ISBNs:
Paperback: 978-0-9877081-6-8
EPUB: 978-0-9877081-7-5
MOBI: 978-0-9877081-8-2
PDF: 978-0-9877081-9-9

Available in paperback and eBook formats from:
www.bewrite.net

Produced by BeWrite Books

Cover Design © Tony Szmuk 2011
Cover Photograph © Sam Smith 2011

about the author

Peter Loney was born in Barrow-in-Furness, Cumbria, in 1944. After a period in London he moved in 1968 to Sarajevo, Former Yugoslavia, where he spent the next twenty years working as an English teacher and freelance translator. Following a prolonged sojourn in New York he returned to Bosnia but as circumstances in the country deteriorated he made his way back to Britain and worked for several years at the World Service in London. He now lives in Ulverston, on the edge of the Lake District in south-west Cumbria.

Leli

Daješ zeleno lišće
Mome stablu od pepela

Vasko Popa

He who stands aloof runs the risk of believing himself better than others and misusing his critique of society as an ideology for his private interests. While he gropingly forms his own life in the frail image of a true existence, he should never forget its frailty, nor how little the image is a substitute for true life.

Theodor Adorno

*To sing is either praise
or defiance. Praise is defiance.*

Margaret Atwood

Contents

Part One

Peninsula
(one: 1-21)

1

To get out you take the A590
To Levens Bridge, turn left for Scotland
And right for England. A curlew's cry
At dusk, stags splashing through saltmarsh, sand
Empty to the horizon. Gulls and redshanks crowded
Along the foreshore as the local train,
Rumbling off the viaduct, pulls in
To Grange. Frontier halt. Weight like gull squalls lifted
As it pulls out again. Arriving
After a week, or years, the same sensation.
Terrain — the old joke's nowhere — cut off from
The mainland, though part of it. An exiled tongue
Where slagbanks crumble in the tide, asylumed
Nib of limestone dipped in the North's ocean.

2

A Rothko triptych: left, *Earth over Green*; right,
Light over Blue; middle, ember-like, an image
of eclipse: red lead ground smeared with lamp-black,
its molten glow frozen — the human spiritual magma?
I had the frame shop guillotine the glossy white
and mount the cropped prints on weightless, frameless
½-inch-thick polystyrene. Spiked on headless pins
knocked through dabs of blu-tack, they adorn the otherwise
blank wall like cloudy or fuzzy existence
philosophies. Booze and mania. Rothko and Lowell.
Late work repeating the same old form. *Black
over Grey*. Scarred carbons. Synthetic polymer. Fatigue
and exemplary failure. *A nihilist has to live...
gazing the impossible summit to rubble.*

3

Work-table, Birkrigg walks ... A reef of seawall
With a ledge of perished bench bolted to it
That smells of the estuary. It's where I sit
Weighing my words — the appraisal
Of my harshest critic's fine ear searching
Each sound. Sand. An ear. A big parched tongue
Whose tip probes inland through viaduct piers
And saltmarshes, into the peninsula's
Miriest fissure. Footprints, hoofprints, tyre-tracks
Wait for obliteration by the tide,
The wandering hieroglyphics great blackbacks
And curlews scratch over the glaze and glitter
Compelling me, compelling me to concede
Where I've erred from or slurred ground and water.

4

Furness might be 'Far-ness', an ore-veined nose
Below the lobe of Iron Age Cumberland
Breathing in Goidelic and Norse
With pollen and spores carried on the wind
Off the Irish Sea and north Atlantic.
Far from *me* - schoolbound, cranking my bike
Under the scar-like slagbank's blank stare.
I might savour roots (scar: *sker* (Norse), or *eskhara,*
From Old Greek 'scab', 'hearth'), but when I turn
I see an ashen blast-furnace-baked face
Among snowy bedsheets, an unknown man,
My grandfather, dying in a room in Askam
In disgrace, his ditched wife, a worse disgrace,
In Lancaster Moor mental asylum.

5

Exemplar?...I see an early photograph
— a child interrupting Dad, the black-and-white
So ill-exposed it's like a negative:
The dacha's bare wood floor, a fog of light,
Pen poised, finger raised (bidding her wait
A beat?) — a withdrawn, concentrated
Affirmation: the disciplined composer at work.
He never budged from there and never spoke.
Hermetically sealed from strangers ('shackled', 'wounded'),
Shostakovich was given what used to be
A hen house... a piano... a kind of table
Nailed to the wall. The Eighth Symphony
Was written (there) ...Remarkably
Nobody ever heard a single sound.

6

Looking across this channel (into which,
When the tide brimmed, red-leaded tanker hulls
Sank amid Lilliputian flotillas
Of wailing tugs) you see a slick of beach
And the prison's sheds like disused hangars.
Gulls scale the quiet over there: a shallow boom
Where the remnant of lifers lingers
On defence contracts. The rest are at home.
Quiz shows, reality, porn, stale documentaries
On Greek coins, great apes, a glimmer of rubble
Thirteen billion light-years from where they sit,
At the edge of existence, coffee tables
Littered with cans, crisp bags, wine empties
Washed up in the wake of benefit.

7

Cold black light... the slaggy dawned on me
Before I dawned. It is escarpment; a low
Massif; the rubble of a volcano.
A charred plateau burying the shore and the sea.
Today out skirting the peninsula
I found a clinker relic like a breakwater
Crumbling in the tide. Home ground. — As though it were
A spur of Walney Road's slag mesa —
That founding image which might underwrite
These late collages. Truncated sun
Standing on the horizon far within.
Verdureless Hissarlik-like heap I've spent
Decades excavating, sifting through twilit
Strata, dwellings, without enlightenment.

8

Mist the colour
Of snow or woodsmoke
In the folds of the low fells.
Slatelight slowly turning
Dew-grey pasture
A saturated green.
GlaxoSmithKline
Fermenting palliatives
Down there near the shore
Adding its pall
To the overcast, burning
To dispel
The sublime limestone vista's
Vacant look.

9

In the Co-op earlier the tills broke down.
While staff tutted and fiddled I heard
Currency tumble by the hour, dishevelled
Girls at our Koševo checkouts break down,
Yoy! Yoy! Helpless to keep up
With the unhinging spiral. Quitting the shops
For the dewy tomb-choked churchyard
On the outskirts, the bench where I sit moored
In stagnant smaragdine light, snaps flooded back
From that pot-holed road-trip before we got out
And roads closed. Our visit to the Patriarchate
In Peć, Vesna uneasy as we looked
At the venerable mulberry-tree in the grounds,
Berries splattered red on the flagstones.

10

'You're standing in my light.' The dormer window,
All filth and cobwebs, illuminates his ghost
In bib-and-brace powdered with sawdust.
Staircarpet ends on the landing below.
A dark, narrow, steep flight and you come up
Between floorboards into redolence.
Chisels, tressle-bench, spirit levels, a workshop's
Linseed and glue reek. Though I is a wee absence —
A shiver, a faint grain — *métier*
Resonated in that resinated space.
Inhaling shavings, stalled... I can't complain
I lack a classical education.
I hear him now, his musical Ulster
Philosophical, *Och, our Peter, he's a dead loss*.

11

A cormorant skims the cappuccino churn
Where the tide's turning against a force ten
Breathing offshore. The ink wings dwindle on
Towards big silt-laden wrinkles driven
Back on the ebb. August is drifting south
Into the now uncharted where
Climate spirals. The bay melts into the mouth
Of an equatorial muddy river
Day after day. I squint and find the tar
Flake of plumage grazing the far
Turmoil of deep water, its ingrained
Road to a now almost expunged horizon
And feel the shingle slip I'm standing on
Anchored together on this exposed headland.

12

I reread this cogent academic, reach out
For the flat red joiner's pencil
Found in the street outside the docks' gate
Like Dad's last trace. Redolent as Proust's mouthful
Of remembrance — wee chewed graphite chisel! —
I scooped it from the pavement and now hold
Both my father and his world
Between my fingers. *James sees that there is*
An inhumanity at the root of art
For all its ardent affirmation of
The human. I flag the whole passage, underline
This with a brush-thick, smudgy horizon.
Black over grey, non-colours Rothko gave
In to as he despaired of representation.

13

Caked clay-white and red but not like clowns,
More like faces from the Mato Grosso
Under the streetlights. Chants, echoes —
A family resemblance to dung-green
And oak-leaf faces... Though the folklore rabble
Who morris and clog on rainy cobble
In Market Street (where post-war tarmac
Was stripped and the resonant mosaic
Restored to boost 'atmosphere') are no match
For this authenticity. Draped in flags,
Pints dripping, they've spilled out in the road to watch
A closing-time fray — hefty legless slags
Scuffling and kicking. One spectator's so canned
He's lost the plot, still yelling 'ENGLAND ENGLAND!'

14

My *oeuvre* slag overcast
Lit by the odd fogged shaft.
Look! inundated waste
And grave-trash — all that's left
Hélas: How autumn's touch
Withers rosy ideas...
— Now spadework! I must ditch
Terrain flooded for years.
Who knows if seeds will find
In ground washed like a shore
Their mysterious kind
Of future? Time! time
Is against me, bluish slime
That silts the aorta.

(Baudelaire: *L'ennemi*)

15

A blur of clamour offshore, drowned in fog,
Desolate and eerie like beings lost
In the swift currents. Not far out and far from lost,
Palavering, in their element, vague
Visitants pierce visibility's
Horizon, crowd the ebb, and melt away.
Wintry dusk. Drizzle. The draining bay's
Whispered *shh*... That wild serenity
However evanescent — divers? red
Throated? great northern? I'll never know —
Adrift, a feathery archipelago
Erupting spume and spray where plumage stood
Unfolding on the shifting wilderness
Like an admonition: *Hush! Witness!*

16

I've shelved his books, existence's founder,
For the time being. Dawn? Twilight? (*For
The Time Being*: Auden's pun as he caved in
To derelict mines and lovingly restored Sin
In the New World.) Instead of *Ecce Homo*, walks,
No, rambles. The boisterous scour of the upland beck
Is his voice: dwindling then inaudible
Shards in the gorge below the lane that ambles
Down to the arterial's standstill. Stop,
Look, listen. Smouldering idly
Both ways: diesel rippling into the air
With noon FM — blurred Mahler, rap, chat. 'I
Too speak of a 'return to nature'...
Not... a going-back... *a going-up...*'

17

Nature is filth. Only the devious strength
which survives is in the right. But that strength itself
is only nature. The whole ingenious machinery
of modern industrial society
is no more than nature dismembering itself.
There is no longer any medium
through which this contradiction can find expression.
It unfolds with the glum obstinacy of a world
from which art, thought, and negativity have vanished.
Human beings are so radically estranged
from themselves and nature that they know only
how to use and harm each other. Each is merely
a factor, the subject or object of some praxis,
something to be reckoned with or discounted.

(Theodor Adorno & Max Horkheimer,
Dialectic of Enlightenment, 1944)

18

Sat on a tomb sheltered from the churchyard's
Harsh sunlight, Smirnoff miniatures tinkling,
My hangover dredging up embalmed shards.
— 'The exhilaration of despair...' It rings
Shallow today. A shade is filling a bag
With the smoky faeces of her overweight dog.
I know her from my walks. No salutation
Today — as though I were a headstone,
A stained angel mutely sounding the last horn...
And we shall be changed. 'A nightmare
Person' a soak who'd known him described Bacon
To me, in a London pub. But he was pissed,
Muddling art and life — works deeply based
In defacement; and cheap 'exhilaration', 'despair.'

19

Fumes of beef and carrot casserole, in
On low since noon. Marcello's oboe's solo
Heiterkeit. Jargon face-down in a yellow
Pyramid of lamplight. Skylight a specimen
Of galaxies splashed with a nebular
Archipelago of ordure. *Bare night*
Is best, bare earth... and this backwater
Apartment above New Market Street's
Failing shops and a booming Bargain Booze.
Immune! My obsolete being brimming
With its own vernacular. *To sing...*
Praise is defiance. Heiterkeit. The word is
Untranslatable. 'Cheerful serenity...
Exuberance... anger... scorn... rhapsody.'

20

The path's last traces have gone.
Only the contractor's
Parallel wooden railings
Commemorate
A buried presence: cambered
And runnelled clay Augusts baked
To a dusty furlong
Of warm terracotta
That would glow in the afternoon
Like an open country road
Brought to light by Corot
Or the russet track
John Clare saw at dawn
Before his world darkened.

21

A day struck like a work from the flurry
And rubble of autumn's back-end, luminous
And stilled; like noon acres near Delft, but free
Of horizon mist and mellowing haze,
The terrain stands bare in its own blaze.
Sobering, though, how scraping at it fails
To graze this indwelling gravity
Even now, scraping *l'automne des idées*.
A shadow across a day without shadows.
This day as echo of a state of mind —
Think that — however fugitively gained.
Think it your hard-won essence, basic stance,
Light flooding ochre and rust woodland, crows
Heightening a stubbled hayfield's radiance.

Interlude: Sheltered Accommodation

> *Nihilism means: Nothing is befalling everything and in every respect.* Martin Heidegger

At eighty-six she sits
Near the telly, only
Her vulnerable sites
Swollen or crippled. I
Indulgently endure
Man. U., *Who Wants to Be*
A Millionaire?, while hours
Crawl, grateful I'm free
Of her and hers: walls rich
In sepulchral photographs
And loud snaps; elsewhere I'd laugh
At the working-class kitsch
On shelves and sill. A meal,
Microwaved junk, will come
And re-heat the indelible
Economy of home.

Her father, Granddad — a blur
The walls don't picture — sat
In the coal-hole corner,
Blackened coat, cap, the white
Linen scarf they all wore
To shield their faces, purred,
Coughed, choked, till a raw
Ghost of a voice whispered
Teatime greetings... Two brothers
Followed at the furnace face,

Both whispered as though
Each lacked a proper voice.
One, Uncle Jim, sank dead
In the red-hot smog. They gave
His wife three-hundred quid
Compensation. Alive,
Her husband, Dad, was just
A thing to them as well,
Biddable, a cost
From the Yard's slate-roofed pool
Of labour. A boy he had
Run Belfast's pavements bare-
Foot. *Och things*, he'd said,
Are grand here since the war.

It's half-time now, time
For tea. Already
The conditioned reflex chimes
Through her frail wintry
Being's dusk. The tremor
In her wasted arms is age.
Anxiety — old fear
Astir still — ravages
Only her eyes and lips,
Unconscious, traceable
To the Slump, the remote whips
And wheels that made her soul.
She limps to the microwave
And dithers. She's afraid
To withhold and to give
Too much. The concentrated,
Pleading look in her eyes
Is the one from cheap shops,
Market-stalls, cheap cafés,
My hand in her tight grip.

Night. Unlit alley. Murmur
And glare from The Anchor.
— Out in fresh damp, inhaling
The backstreet chill ... Striding
Out under stars, passing
Boarded-up shops, pub door
Applause. The streets are dark,
Emptier than when
They led home. At the relic
By the stop — CORONATION
GARDENS — I wait to get
The late bus out to my
Fell-sheltered market
Town domicile. Indigo sky,
A big ochre moon,
Like the one Wordsworth saw
Over Windermere,
Shedding weird light on
Sheds for the Trident programme
They scrapped... Gifted, lucky
Beneficiary
Of unearned income
How he'd have loved this sight.
I know that what they say
Is right, right, right — from Marx
To Adorno — *dans le vrai*
About exchange and ex-
Ploitation, estrangement, de-
Humanisation. Though
Concerns have changed now,
The poorest see
A big difference.
So what should I do? Join
The Fabian Society?
EarthFirst!? Get a gun?

Peninsula
(22-43)

22

A flutter glimpsed along the beck
Glimmers thrush-dark, like the water,
And lights on a shoal. Wait though... Arctic
White below — a rare visitor!
Down there in the stony gorge
Among boulders and swabbling pour
The earth-plumaged dipper's polar
Shirt's an augur. I touch the bridge
For luck, fingering warm limestone
Like Rilke's tower: knocking on,
This is a first and last sighting
Most likely. See... the stranger's waded
Into and right under the spring
Deluge, searching bedrock for food.

23

Not tomorrow. Cracks show it will take
The Greenland ice sheet generations to melt.
Though poetry's torso already grows opaque
And lustreless as Thalassarctos' pelt
Yellowing in Natural History.
Why does Nietzsche's *Beyond* feel *passé*
His critical incandescence notwithstanding?
Shut your eyes, recapture the dawn tang
Of snowed-in Sils Maria... Nostalgia
For avalanched high valleys in the settled past?
No... more like nostalgia for the future.
Ironic how this morning echoes his
Chance collapse: dementia, paralysis,
While tomorrow is steadily effaced.

24

One for sorrow, two for joy. Magpies
Up from a ditch ash, hang, drop like dice
To fogged pasture, among downcast eyes
Of cattle, grazing, blind to folk-auguries.
Grass... *a green silence.* 'Joy', 'sorrow' —
Why do these words feel somehow out of date?
Like poeticisms? I watched them in sub-zero
Shiveringly commemorate
The site's liberation, while grandchildren
Frisked children at checkpoints. No, despite
Intuitions of obsolete diction,
I recite aloud to the birds the less ornate,
Grittier, jaundiced, more down-to-earth
Northern, *One for anger, two for mirth.*

(27. Ol. 05.)

25

Along the foreshore's pebble-grey and rose
Before dark. A dying hearth. Herons shake
Aloft from rosé shallows like flakes
Of hot ash. A wavering blizzard of redshanks
Wafts off shrieking up the tideline, snows
Back into the surf. Far out, drizzling flocks
Colonise the sandbanks, swelling up now
Like atolls over inundated shadows.
Flecks of magma, shore crows
Patrol the mud under a slag headland.
Above them the big cooling ember glows,
A stone-cold memory. The mouth's imbued,
The shallow fells steeped. A speck in oilskins draws
A wake across the ebb with reddened oars.

26

So still... it might be a driftwood stake
Planted gratuitously on the shore.
— Too far to tell gender. Gargoyles and spires
Of their retreat's Victorian pile poke
Above its sublime, run-down arboretum
Where I — the grounds aren't closed — and they explore
The pathos of awe. Nature's defaced there
Not honoured, as this estranged soul would claim.
But what difference now? I see them in town,
In stores, queuing at the wall, maroon
Habits, shaved heads, vowels from Maine and Sheffield.
A thousand feet apart on hissing shingle
The pair of us stand and gaze, our stances failed
Antipodes of dissent and denial.

27

What is sacred — trashed word? — *trashed* — the back
Of this bloke's head shaved like a camp inmate's
And livid with swastikas? Post-glacial Black
Coomb's silhouette under its slate
And rose cap of dusk-stilled cumulus?
— Rehearsing this issue on the district bus
Where issues surface and sink issuelessly
Like in the closed world of a Beckett play.
A clearing opened for a time, hoary, shaftlit,
To naive philosophasters like me,
Identical with but not nature:
A scraped skull scarred with ancient graffiti,
The beach's phosphorescent twilight,
Being, Heidegger's word, its desecrator.

28

Watching a kestrel dangle on Hampstead Heath,
Years ago, hearing Hopkins probably —
Who watched havoc boom — an old hippie on the path,
Pointing, said, 'It means the land's healthy.'
Buzzards... hawks, curlews, snipe: the boggy moor's bonus.
Today though searching a rig's light I saw
The moteless sky above the Towers of Silence...
Remains without vultures. Radio Four
Spoke of the 'carrion stench...' I turn away
To poetry local as beck-water,
Compacted and fissured like the peninsula's
Limestone strata, where catastrophe
Is clouds on the dusk skyline, not a sun
Already standing clear of the horizon.

29

Faked verdigris from head to toe
Except where bronze sinews show through
Like bark, he fingers V-shaped pipes
Like two slender bottles of hock
Held neck to neck. His pitted prick
Is a hilt, the blade buried deep
Emerging brittle and decayed
Like a Mycenaean treasure
As bestial tail. Ouzo, retsina
And the ruins! Brimming I paid
A wad for this green wraith of health.
Sacred, his pipes rise overhead.
The crushed spines of the vintage dead
Below him, crowding my bookshelf.

30

The modern ocean is no longer
The primordial Eden revealed to 19th century
Oceanographers. Frock-coats, clouds of hair,
Like Marx or Darwin doubles. Even Nietzsche,
The deepest listener whose soundings first heard
Impoverishment echoing in fished-out grounds,
Lacked our horizon — scope to track a marine bird
Gliding for months on end towards
Extinction. A sea change. *As Conrad knew*
The sea will never go back... In the long run
Man-made imbalances will settle into
New evolutionary equilibria,
Which may not be to man's taste or
Advantage. Eventually the sea will win.

31

To a child returning from a holiday, home
seems new, fresh, festive. Yet nothing
has changed there since he left. Only because duty
has now been forgotten, of which each piece
of furniture, window, lamp, was otherwise a reminder,
is the house given back this Sabbath peace,
and for minutes one is at home in a never-returning
world of nooks, rooms and corridors in a way
that makes the rest of life there a lie. No
differently will the world one day appear,
almost unchanged, in its constant feast-day light,
when it stands no longer under the law
of labour, and when for home-comers
duty has the lightness of holiday play.

(Theodor Adorno, 1945)

32

Another rosy sunrise probes the room,
Floods my stack. The week's beginning deadmarch
Is mote-shafts, black tea, fagsmoke's bluish bloom
Stirring, untroubled by the Shostakovich
Violin concerto, pitched to wake the dead.
(The girl below has gone to work, I heard
Our backstreet door slam). This is solitude
As Buber illumined it, the lustrous side
Of lonely existence — abjuring strict
Rules of engagement, job, web, TV, cellphone,
Exhilarated sitting here alone
Listening to Dmitri's harsh verdict
Resonate, like Buber's *The Eclipse of God*,
That darkening, the Monday morning mood.

33

The tiller tingles as we *put-put* out
Past derelict slips, sheds, high-tech ochre
Assembly shops. — South, towards the offshore
Gas-rig blockade which litters the slate-
Blue sound's mouth: *Sea Jade* and me *Au fond
de l'inconnu pour trouver du nouveau!*
— Another loose end in a language I don't know.
And it's too late now, ankle-deep among
The trash and bladderwrack of Walney beach,
Sea Jade's bilge awash with shingle like
A giant *objet trouvé:* ebb-drenched, bleached
And splintered, her peeling timbers sharp
As regret ... Treacherous waters... Was my ship
Once fresh with tar and the sea wine-dark?

34

Ex-cityite, I love the name,
Its poetry — *limestone pavement.*
These outcrops of old sea bottom
Unhinge my view of the present
Sahara floor, sienna now
As the glazed acres bake bone-dry
To a hazy crust, miles below.
Up here it's light, salt air, stone, sky,
Where afternoon quiet's a stratum
Tunnelled by lonely skylarks. I'm
Away! — as far as I can walk
From footprints sunk in a flagstone
Where poor Princip shot the archduke
In the thin time we call human.

35

Landfall? Enough?... I'm dreaming Ithaca.
My daughter smokes roll-ups on her hardwood deck
Watching spring's raid ignite upstate New York,
Her siren-call relayed by optical fibre.
'*Peninsula* will keep...' A satellite
Kindles the ocean, Lowell's great green go-light.
'And besides, the reality's a shit-
Hole promontory *Bogu iza ledja.*'
A squall of April hail and skylights blur.
Behind God's back... — A break from lying art
And this myth of nowhere, itself absurd?
— Yes! Go! Revisit Tompkins County's Wal-Mart
And perish from the truth! Departure! bags, trains, flight-
Terminal vodkas, the great iron bird!

36

Oriana: 'A floating luxury hotel'
Berthed at the fitting-out dock. Dad's on his knees
On the grand staircase's timbers. Polaris,
A grimy chrysalis, idles,
Klieg-lit, cradled under tarps, her safe-thick
Shell still littered with my chalky prints.
— Those cold hulls! Bellied and arced sediment
Distilled from the slaggy! — Perversely, I think,
I'm writing its elegy. I watched red bloom
Above the tip, rose after fuming rose,
And drain from starless dark like an omen.
Years on contractors began to strip
The pile away in truckfuls for
Road building and a base for fertiliser.

37

A latte-coloured woman slumbers in just
A soiled Giant's T-shirt, face down
In a sidewalk arcade on the Lower West
Side, off Broadway, in downtown's dense noon,
Like a piece of garbage amongst the garbage.
42nd Street porn is come of age,
Poverty witnessed by impoverishment's
Inured first citizens, Enlightenment's
Mature flora. Nobody's abashed to look
Or to avert their eyes from this sad fuck.
Nietzsche savoured a wild hope: we'll translate
'The terrible basic text *homo natura*'
Back into nature. Utopian even before
Corruptions introduced by Wall Street.

38

The limestone's outermost extremity
Where sealight's oyster void stands open
Flooding the bus with marine buoyancy.
The tide's out. Bleached rose, ultramarine,
And zinc-white hulls litter the saltmarsh
Below the causeway. We are departing Rampside
Where the guillotine's short-lived rumble and crash
Settled Wordsworth's mind. I love this dyke-road
Out to Roa Island's wheelhouse-like bar
Though I know already how things will be
— Stale, the saloon a morgue where I'll stare
Through ribbed panes, under the gibbering telly
Telling me it's too late, futile to believe
In the sea and boats, any alternative.

39

I have not shifted
but I am not there
any more let them in let them look
around search the rib shadowed water
mill grinds ripe emptiness stumps
of cheap dreams smoulder
in the ashtray I am not there the moored boat
undulates in the aorta a couple
of unripened words hang
in my cloudy throat
I am not there any longer I
have not shifted but already
I am far away surely too
far for them now

(Vasko Popa, *Odlazak)*

40

From a café's upper-floor window-seat
The long view down awninged Cavendish Street,
Fringe of a backstreet utopia
Bulldozed last century. There, matinée
Inspired — Crazy Horse and Custer, Nazis
And English — we lived the dialectical
Life of imagination. The mouth of the alley
Is still there, from which — *Geronimo!* — we'd spill,
A tatterdemalion tribe among
The teatime shoppers. Wilderness already wrong
Before we were out of school and in school ink
Indentured in history. Today I know
Only that it is deep folly to think
Utopia; deeper folly not to.

41

At the bottom of Ainslie Street I sheered left
Instead of right and quit the working day.
While buses nudged into the dismayed army —
A dawn swarm on foot and bikes — my two-stroke coughed
Through chestnut-lit outskirts to the abbey ruins.
Thanks to the place, blessings upon the hour.
This morning I stood where I stumbled on
Enlightenment's edge. The architecture
Is still unfallen rubble — torn walls, black
In sunrise's shadows, dusty rose
In the sharp light. Echoes of long ago's
Truant dawn: the far-off boom of work
And my reading that nothing's written in
The hive's reverberation or sandstone.

42

A new Shostakovich *Life*, too technical
For me — again though a fogged snap I like
— With Nina, stretched clothed on a shore. Some pebble
Moraine in another time zone where music
Is still at stake. And here's Rothko's *The Artist's*
Reality: Philosophies of Art. At least
This earnest, plodding screed was written
Before he hit his stride and struck a vein.
I chuck it aside and contemplate his three
Mature sonnets fastened to my wall: blurred, groundless
Shapes upon groundless grounds... This piece
Is beginning to sound like an Apology
From the ditch. So what? Whatever! — like Malone
Inventorising, 'I know what I mean.'

43

I am back in boyhood, chilled, wading through
The darkest stretch of Cocken Tunnel
Under the slaggy. I can only dimly feel
The immense cake of sediment I know
I am buried beneath. The tunnel's stones
Sweat under its weight. A dripping silence
Eerily denies my presence.
Still remote, the shore-lit mouth beckons.
But when I get to it there is no shore
Littered with muck and rubble off the tip
But water, blue-grey, swamping the lip
Of the tunnel, a thunderous swell and furor
Exploding spray against the clinker scree.
That and the weight and darkness have stayed with me.

Part Two

Domicile

Pitter... The skylight murmurs. Mutters. Wait...
Now clatter. Desk and workroom resonate.

*

For days roofs ripple, shed curtains of rain,
Or blaze through amnesties of smoky sunshine.

*

Out in the lanes farm buildings stand like tide-
Exposed wrecks in thin lakes thick with seabirds.

*

Estuary... Viaduct ... The open bay —
Washed out. A train's rumble. A wader's cry.

*

The swollen pour of Dragley Beck
Through weirs of Tesco trolleys, beer-crates, estate dreck.

*

The drenched moor. The drying road. The rich
Soiled speech: downpour spouting into the ditch.

*

At last! after weeks of it, blurry sleet
Furs the roofs and slowly silts Market Street.

*

A still night. Stars sprinkle the slanted panes
While breaths from Arkhangelsk blanch the Pennines.

*

Air smells wintry now. Between bare hills
The pikes and shoulders of the snowlit fells.

*

Beige-mottled cygnets, big now. The reed-swamp
Frost camouflages their long-cold heap.

*

Kestrels search the moor for life. Even
The great blades are stilled, above bleached terrain.

*

Hoarfrost. The untouched landscape. Dull reports
Across stubble acres melt like fingerprints.

*

Slag-grey ice. Air thrums. Snowy beings
Land, glissando... Canal choked with wings!

*

The pasture's scab has thawed overnight
And hedgerows enclose fields flooded with light.

*

The estuary shading out, becoming the bay.
A slate dusk. Waders wade in mercury.

Memento

Brittle now, in a cracked vodka tumbler
The wisp of moor still smoulders on the sill.
Its sinew of torn stem's evolved a caul
Of emerald slime, bark has dyed the water
To beery murk. Upland fragrance
And colours long gone, last September's spray —
Heather, ling ... *Calluna vulgaris?* — still dimly
Commemorates some last rite of abstinence.

Old fears and gutter nostalgia stir.
Mixed with the memory of bracken's forlorn
Spreading oxblood stain smell the red
Institutional blanket, see the water
Clear, the glass become a ward's old-fashioned
Drip-stand bottle hanging upside-down.

Lepenski Vir

I

Ages they've incubated in my head
Since our cultural foray that July.
Stone eggs. Fish-faced boulders shore mud buried.
They're hatching ... Archaic rubble, augury.

Refurbished Turk- and *Wehrmacht*-wrecked Old
Serbian Orthodox monasteries —
Focus of Vesna's Nikon — blue and gold
Narrative walls where flaked paint freezes

Intelligible myths of church and state,
Dimmed when our book- and map-choked Renault 4
Topped wooded scarp above the Iron Gate.
Below, eroding the old gorge floor,

A zigzag lake that is the Danube
Stalled by the Djerdap dam. Adrift, we idled down
To take in the salvaged nub
Of a freak dawn in Europe (the dam drowned

The proto-neolithic site; but, like a cake,
Professors and navvies had sliced and hauled
To an upper niche the ground of that 'unique
And isolated vision of the world').

II

I enter the amber underwater light
Shed by corrugated fibreglass
Awnings — heightening the *unheimlichkeit*
Eight thousand years impart to the place.

Unearthed by stunned hands under humdrum
Starchevo strata, the shrine-dwellings' red
And blackish haematite floors fan out from
The cliffs of their reconstructed beach. 'Truncated

Isosceles triangles...' Enlightening texts fail
At this failed site. Geometrical
Identity, a vexing, eerie
Composite of symmetry and mystery

Is all that's left, as if
Ground plan, threshold slabs, flagged shrine and hearth-pit
Had blueprinted a solitary hieroglyph,
The whole of a lost tongue's alphabet.

III

Stone-gilled, fish-lipped boulders, they've swum
Up out of thick murk. Exhausted,
They gasp and stare in strip-lighted
Tanks in the stark site museum.

From the Shrine-Dwelling Under
The Rock. 'Europe's first monumental
Sculptures.' However cast our cool
Net falls short: *Danubius, Sirena...*

They witnessed the Neolithic
Revolution behind cold hearths
Which slowly filled with sand and muck
Their big round eyes and downturned mouths.

IV
Exhumed and refurbished
these stanzas from years ago
might get my censor's stamps,
Imago, Stet,

with this postscript.
— Little soapstone memento
bought at the site
your blank stare is now

a paperweight. Yet behind
your carp's muzzle
and big blind eyes
there lingers a freshwater

trace of primordial dreams
and bestial credence.
In my mind's eye
I see it just

as it might have been. Dawn
hearth-smoke enshrouding
the shrine-dwellings, figures
in hides and furs

assembling by the river
with nets, hooks, antler
tools for the bloodbath.
Just as it was. Red

flags, swollen
banners, Marshal Tito Street
thick with crowds
negligently celebrating

Brotherhood and Unity.
Before accumulated
floodwater
inundated all in

the name of whatever...
Sanguinity... Soil...
Kultura... Some smoking
midden of myth.

Du Soir

These dusks the ling-spray trembles on my sill;
Each minute bloom exhales its upland smell
Lost in the disintegrating air down here:
Spiralling fag-smoke, a late sonata.

Each minute bloom exhales its upland smell.
The keyboard's thunder brings you near.
Spiralling fag-smoke, a late sonata,
Coagulating clouds, *rouge*, beautiful.

The keyboard's thunder brings you near
Though I now abhor your toxic *noir*.
Coagulating clouds, *rouge*, beautiful,
As the sun disintegrates in its own pall.

Though I now abhor your toxic *noir*,
And the years lost in you, I remember it all...
As the sun disintegrates in its own pall
You thunder in me like a closing bar.

(Baudelaire: *Harmonie du Soir*)

Nil by Mouth

(Sign hung above the bed)

My head's full of hospital. Mam's dying.
Or she'll glimmer through nine days' recovery —
Lucid, herself again, her left side wrong
A bit, perhaps, her speech blurred — only
For total eclipse on the tenth. That's how
This angel of effacement operates.

Ashen grimace above the snowy sheets —
Like her father in Askam all those years ago —
She's dead to the world, or with ill-focussed
Seer's eyes, in parched words, she tells me
What a tense time we had yesterday
When Scunthorpe lost to Aston Villa — just!
And how, up the Abbey in the afternoon
With Phyllis — and dad was there — and Jacqueline
(How *quiet* it was), we picnicked in the green
Amphitheatre opposite
The ruins. When in fact she was out of it,
Slumped, undiscovered till eight-fifteen,
Her big recliner in front of the telly
Sopping.

                    So I just sit there like a shard
Of slag amongst the twilit technology,
The selfish, hardhearted son (*Oh, you're so hard*)
Who shared nothing with them, never shed a tear.
Though I did cry once, I'd like to tell her,
When I used her as an emblem — no,
Embodiment — of capital's *sine*
Qua non: material and spiritual
Impoverishment of that historical
Curio: the wretched proletariat.

I was stalled at a crux of the rough draft
When they welled, big midden-soiled sobs that left
Me choking, unswallowable as the bright
Puréed pap the nurses tested her with.
What I was so harrowed about is both —
Like poetry itself — mysterious
And plain as the backyard wall of our ur-home
In bomb-rubbled Preston Street. That heartless poem,
Dry-eyed later drafts regardless,
Closed for a spell the light-years-deep crevasse
That opens between us and our buried selves.

The nurses are hard, like me, but sweet
With it, and leave us lingerers on alone.
So I just sit there, knowing it's too late
To say those things I never would have said
In any case, my ink-stained
Right hand holding her limp left one.

Towpath *Capriccio*

After a May of rain and autumn gales
June's palette-knife has restored the hawthorns
To heavily chalked green along the canal's
Embankment, to clear echoes in its lagoon's

Flawless Venetian mirror. — More Guardi,
Though, than Canaletto. Camped beside the tarmac,
Tattooed blokes with lavish tackle, TVs
And twelve-packs fish for pike they'll throw back.

Homage to a Bad Spaniard

Don't you suppose — since I am in a confidential and confessional vein — that when they have accused me of not being a good Spaniard I have often said to myself: "I am the only Spaniard: I — not these other men who were born and live in Spain."

*

To the isolated, isolation seems an indubitable certainty; they are bewitched on pain of losing their existence, not to perceive how mediated their isolation is.

The first — old ravishing gem! — is an epigraph
by Miguel Unamuno, author of
The Tragic Sense of Life — planted flag-like
by the seditious inner-exile,
writer and poet, Alexander Trocchi
in *Cain's Book* (1959), for me
a work that resonated like a call.

Half-awake, callow, chronically embryonic
poet, and *soi-disant* Disaffected
Outsider, immersed in what would come to be known
to the West — and me — as 'the Sixties phenomenon',
I was working in a musty organic-food shop
in swinging London's Notting Hill Gate
when — Christ! — Cain himself walked in
trailed by a laughing caftan'd woman and a troop
of rowdy children. It was like coming
face to face with Genet or Beckett.

The Clyde eddying
in his voice, this was the Hudson River
Ishmael who had written, *Extreme
predicaments, if I do not bore the reader
with such a frivolous topic, call for extreme
measures of adaptation...*

Thereafter
I'd glimpse him passing by, a horse-bleached wraith
hunched against W11's psychedelic rain,
or out of it in the pub, amidst the profound
frivolity. One noon I saw him descending
the steps into the Gate Underground
never to be seen or heard from again.

The second's Adorno, author of
The Culture Industry, again an epigraph —
to one of his last books about Spain.

On the Afternoon Train

to Lela, *again*

You give green leaf
To my tree of ashes
            Vasko Popa

Arcing south towards you
through acres of August's basking rubble
the felled hayfields are the colour
that you dye your hair.

From there it's no distance
to my own dull grey shock
and colourless dwelling on
velocity, destination.

Till I remember how
you shaved below for
our shuttered spell by a shimmer
of Dalmatian shore,

an undulation
pale amidst scorched
terrain, soft karst,
a moonlit dune...

Lines written and
the Quiet Zone suddenly fresh
with *ruzmarin*
and the tang of brine.

Trophy

*Mystical explanations are considered deep. The truth is that they
are not even superficial.* F.W. Nietzsche

Destitute?... The mineral bleakness of
The beach exposed by the receding tide
In the silting light of late afternoon
Speaks my mind in the inimitable tone
Nature assumes. *Abide, abide
Here, by this, your ground, beyond belief*

Is what I might be thinking, words, poetry.
And, mostly submerged, deep, like Wadhead Scar —
The stony undulation starting to nudge
Above the ebb like natural wreckage —
Something unthinkable yet clear
To apprehension, a spiritual trophy

However negative. The Scar's limestone
Rubble's a slick at first. The shadow dries
To emerald weed and boulders, clarifies
To a freak island exposed daily to this
Littoral's radiance, whispering, *That there is
No consolation is your consolation.*

Climate Change

WC2. Dawn gloom. The rush-hour building.
I came up from Holborn Underground
after 20 years abroad, having wangled
a low-grade job through a Sarajevo
crony from pavement café days. Still taken aback
by the barbarism: the elderly cast-off who,
settled at rock bottom, was stoically making
her cardboard bed, like a troglodyte,
under Kingsway's cliff of commercial bedrock.
Fur-shawled, stony-faced, aloof from the clans
still slumbering huddled on marble
and granite steps all along the street.
She knelt there daily, ringed by crumpled beercans,
coins, and cellophane-wrapped offerings
from a volunteer lorry. Like a sybil
in her cave: while the morning traffic
thickened she waited for me to stop and ask
what's happening, going to happen.

* * *

I ripped news spewing from the antiquated
teleprinters, rasps like grating masonry,
as the Wall came down. All night and next day
there was wild celebration among the newsroom crowd
as though they themselves had been liberated.
Soon, among dense-print Human Interests, I found
an emaciated urban woman scrabbling for potatoes,
with bare hands, in a wilderness
of black earth, along with hundreds like her.
You heard the gangmaster mutter — between the lines,
gutturals that rose from below the horizon —
that she could take more if she'd let him fuck her.

* * *

Hushed newsroom. Slow-news day. I am standing between
two banks of idle teleprinters
in the cramped telex unit. A sputter of small-arms
and the peace is breached. A bulletin flagged
URGENT. A lull till the cataclysm
or garbage hits the other agencies... Then
I'm ducking about in the deafening crossfire.

* * *

It was mad — hard to credit — like something rigged
when first Reuters, then AP stuttered out
his homely name with for me its perverse
aura of nostalgia. Old pal and Koševo neighbour
from round the corner (I saw our street,
as yet undefaced by rubble and craters).
Fellow poet... I recalled his thatch
of backwoodsman's hair. His stiff spotless doctor's coat,
that crumpled when he sat down opposite
me in the clinic ('*Pazi*, stop so much
to drink...'), nothing like a butcher's apron.

* * *

The twelve-hour shift; spacious Thames-side walks
at break times; radiant, rainless days
deep into autumn — or is that just an ex-
expat's hindsight? It was intoxicating
being back. Plane-trees glittered
on the traffic-choked Embankment, the river
eddied and stalled among blackened pillars
under Hungerford Bridge, re-ignited, swirled
through the daily tide-surge. Idle rush-hour evenings
watching the crimson and chlorophyll chemistry
of the Thames sky, while homecoming starlings'
minatory thunder darkened the air

as they swarmed down, like spiral nebulae
above the dusk melée, onto Westminster
and City roosts. And that Christmas-day vista,
eerie and magical (we'd been mini-cabbed in
for the shift, on treble time — in the canteen
turkey with all the trimmings). From Waterloo Bridge
London deserted, silent, like in some post-
event film, the Thames unruffled, its glaze
grazed by marauding cormorants. A single
car, an old banger trailing exhaust,
detonated along the Embankment, past
moored sightseeing vessels and Cleopatra's Needle —
the rosy-rubble spike clearly visible,
aglow in the sun above a rusting barge.

* * *

I had to be philosophical, aware
from day one the unit wouldn't survive
rationalisation (it was an ideal berth
for writing: 3 days on / 3 off, and with
time to read — Heidegger, Nietzsche — while the garbage
and cataclysms piled up and toppled
off the machines and rolled across the floor
like papyri in a vandalised temple).
It came in ripples: ashen-olive
screens ignited, crashed. Soon though the newsroom
glimmered with sealight as it came on-stream
and we were history. One by one
teleprinters fell silent. The shift
shrank — forced retirements, redundancies. I hung on —
silence, cunning, my now straitened parole —
while the newsroom stilled to a glazed pool
of stargazers, watching the global market swell
like a red giant, the cosmos collapse. The panelled lift,
sinking to Reception and Security, hung

suspended in a genteel time. There was
a trace of déjà-vu, hints of *lacrimae*
rerum in the rows of machines left standing
under ripped typewriter hoods, typewriters
piled like end-of-an-era wreckage
against the unit's back wall.
                          On Kingsway
there were fewer sleeping-bags and blankets (I knew
what was coming down everywhere
during that spell at 'the heart of things'). A salvage
operation was at work: the 'public eyesores'
were being dispersed from the pavements into
hostels, abandoned council blocks and other
hopeless temporary accommodation.

Heathen

Straddling ditch-ice between
Narrow tarmac
And the moor's moraine of frost,
I'm a rag exhaling fog

After that last gradient.
Tundra undulates north
To cloudless cobalt
Where Cambrian rubble, felled

Back in the prehistoric,
Glitters like graphite. My back
Turned on shoulders
Reclaimed for grazing

Behind piled miles
Of drystone wall, I savour
This unyielding terrain.
Hoared bog, bracken rust, heather,

Deemed the wilds. Its wind-
Turbines in today's
Lull unstirred, masts freezing
Fast in the deepening chill.

On Quarry Brow

i

Still weird to find myself up here again
Surveying the peninsula's dead end.
The slagbank desecrated now, like aerial
Footage of a strip-mined mesa. How it's all
Etched — slate roofed miles, then seawashed slag ... And
The faint water-mark, Man, on the skyline.

ii

A dead end, beneath me — that's how I read
The terrain, stood up here years ago
On trips home, viewing the unexcavated slaggy.
Art is the sedimented history
Of human misery. A view I didn't know
Back then, a hard sentence I hadn't read.

iii

Beneath? ... Left behind? No, more like beyond me
As, wrenched free, I floundered to locate
Radiant ground. Heidegger's toxic sludge
Glittered like a destination. Outrage?...
It took Adorno, that sophisticate,
For slag, slag's fertile negativity.

iv

Suddenly transported: Sedrenik, snow
Thawing from red and ochre roofs spilled
Over the sides of the narrow-floored crevasse.
Bleakness awakening to spring promise.
Howitzers and mortars parked along that road
And rubble drifting in the streets below...

v

I bus down to Barrow, this aporia,
To feed Mam (you can't trust those sweet nurses
Run ragged through shit-
And canteen-scented stroke wards to meet
Efficiency fetishes in the NHS's
Emaciated phantasmagoria)

vi

But stray up here first to look and rehearse,
On the outskirts' edge, where peripheral
Paved streets dwindle into country lanes,
Before going in to her damaged brain's
Tentative mimicry of my smile
Which visits her face like a frightened stranger's.

vii

Does it matter that I've changed my mind
On what matters, what's at stake? Prosaic heat
Prescinds man, 'Being's poem', read through a prism
Of congealing lyrical nihilism.
Orpheus chilled? Have I evolved a blind spot
For light, see just its infra red end?

viii

— The shaft of radiant matter standing offshore,
Between surface glitter and the overcast
It broke moments ago like a rebuke,
Notwithstanding. Photons are in the dark
Whether it's a sea of tranquil dust
Or the rough field of Irish Sea out there.

ix

Only I alone and you alone
Care. Together, what's to us a pillar
Of marine light beyond the 'standing reserve'
That's falling. The slaggy might survive...
Tidewashed, a black atoll, its lunar
Screes blanching with guano as auks return.

x

Anarchist cells, invisible insurrections,
Belong to palaeontology,
With crumbling divine grounds, while the febrile
Ideology which stoked this local hill,
Disfiguring local lives, locality,
Cools and thickens and darkens and hardens

xi

Into superstition. Everywhere being
Scrolls down brokers' screens. The bottom line
Is slag. Pompeian dusk behind Black Coomb...
And she would be waiting if she knew what time
It is now. No rush... I'll go down via the disused lane
That still smells of crab-apples and dung.

Heart with a Dirty Windshield
by Howie Good

"Howard Good turns words into a reciprocating saw that can be worked through your gut. He has internalised the existential horror of existence and turned it outward."

Nathan Tyree

"Howie Good's poetry sleeps with your wife and mocks you in front of your friends. It smokes your last cigarette and hides the remote before spending your grandmother's Social Security check on brightly menacing tattoos. Howie Good's poetry, the reader suspects, works for the Yakuza."

Jason Cook

"Howie Good's poetry remakes reality with startling images, disquieting insights and unexpected juxtapositions. The effect is by turn surreal, disconcerting and always compelling."

Juliet Wilson

"Good's poetry is concerned with the anxious, mad beauty of a perilous dream, and his poems teeter on the precipice of something steep, intimating the threat of a drop down a dangerous abyss. Sometimes wry, sometimes tender, and always urgent, Good's body of work comprises the collective spirit of art in the 21st century. Continuing in the tradition of Breton, Good constructs a dialectic of human history and the nuances of the heart, and locates the tradition of both in the present moment with the lyric as fuel to move his engine forward."

Cynthia Reeser

paperback ISBN: 978-1-906609-47-4
ebook ISBNs: 978-1-906609-48-1

Also Available from BeWrite Books:

And For My Next Trick
by Brian Rosenberger

"With his twists and turns in poems like "Spaghetti Sauce" and "The Tenth Commandment" Brian Rosenberger is the modern-day Saki of the poetry world. In "9 to 5" he dumps on the workplace ("the suicide crawl of the second hand"). In "State of Decay" (ï¿½a tattoo that seemed a good idea at the time") he mourns the waste of his intellect. In the powerful "You Don't Hear the One that Hits You" a lost love is compared to Russian roulette. Rosenberger can be hilarious, as in "By Pork Possessed", or deep, as in the title poem, but he's always right in your face. Whether you like it, or not."

Cindy Rosmus:
editor Yellow Mama, author of collections:
Angel of Manslaughter, Gutter Balls, Calpurnia's Window, and No
Place Like Home.

"...spiked with poisoned puns and acid alliteration... Rosenberger's blamk verse wriggles with imagery as witty as it is disreputable."

Ramsey Campbell

paperback ISBN: 978-1-906609-32-0
ebook ISBNs: 978-1-906609-33-7

Also Available from BeWrite Books:

Cerebral Stimulation
by A. Gregory Frankson

Poetry meant for the page uses imagery and metaphor to speak its universal truths, while spoken word uses performance to captivate, animate and teach. Cerebral Stimulation showcases the gritty realities and emotional tableaux of that rarest of poets - one that shines as brightly on the page as on the stage. This premiere collection of works from one of Canada's emerging poetic talents is destined to become a hallmark of the next generation of African-Canadian literature.

paperback ISBN: 978-1-905202-32-4
ebook ISBNs: 978-1-905202-33-1

BeWrite Books
www.bewrite.net